Creating a Bird-Friendly Backyard Habitat

Scott Edwards

Photo Credits:

Ron Austing: *p. 3 (Red-headed Woodpecker); 4; 5 (Yellow-rumped Warbler); 31 (Pyrrhuloxia); 34; 36; 37; 39 (Yellow Warbler); 40; 50; 51 insert (Butterfly Weed); 52T; 53TC; 54TC (Black-capped Chickadee); 55BC (Red-breasted Nuthatch)*
Jeff Fishbein: *p. 55B*
Kaytee Products: *p. 18; 19T; 22; 25 all; 30; 53B*
Larry Kimball: *p. 9 (Broad-tailed Hummingbird); 12; 21 (Scrub Jay); 27; 32T; 52B*
Larry Kimball & Barbara Magnuson: *p. 46B*
Peter LaTourrette: *p. 8; 54BC; 59*
Barbara Magnuson: *p. 10; 47*
Rafi Reyes: *p. 7; 16T; 17 T & C; 38; 42; 45T; 49C*
Rob & Ann Simpson: *p. 1 (American Goldfinch); 11; 13 (Carolina Chickadee); 32B; 43; 44 all; 45B; 46T; 49T; 52T; 53BC; 54T; 55T (Hairy Woodpecker); 55TC; 56; 57 (Northern Bobwhite)*
Dr. Zoltan Takacs: *p. 6*
John Tyson: *p. 20; 23; 26; 29; 51; 52C; 54B (Tufted Titmouse); 60; 61; 62*
Maleta M. Walls: *p. 16C & B; 17B; 19B; 35; 41; 49B*

KT 102

Distributed in the UNITED STATES to the Pet Trade by T.F.H. Publications, Inc., 1 TFH Plaza, Neptune City, NJ 07753; on the Internet at www.tfh.com; in CANADA by Rolf C. Hagen Inc., 3225 Sartelon St., Montreal, Quebec H4R 1E8; Pet Trade by H & L Pet Supplies Inc., 27 Kingston Crescent, Kitchener, Ontario N2B 2T6; in ENGLAND by T.F.H. Publications, PO Box 74, Havant PO9 5TT; in AUSTRALIA AND THE SOUTH PACIFIC by T.F.H. (Australia), Pty. Ltd., Box 149, Brookvale 2100 N.S.W., Australia; in NEW ZEALAND by Brooklands Aquarium Ltd., 5 McGiven Drive, New Plymouth, RD1 New Zealand; in SOUTH AFRICA by Rolf C. Hagen S.A. (PTY.) LTD., P.O. Box 201199, Durban North 4016, South Africa; in JAPAN by T.F.H. Publications. Published by T.F.H. Publications, Inc.

Manufactured in the
United States of America
by T.F.H. Publications, Inc.

Contents

Any backyard habitat can be made to attract more birds by supplying food, water, and shelter.

Introduction

What is Habitat?

Habitat is the single most important feature of attracting birds and other wildlife to a backyard. Simply put, habitat is a place to live that provides the basic essentials of any living creature's life: food, water, and shelter. With a minimal amount of time and effort, each of these elements can easily be provided in our own backyards.

Because birds are some of the most diverse and adaptable creatures on the planet, bird habitat can consist of many different things. Birds can be found in virtually any habitat on earth; they live and thrive in the subzero temperatures of the South Pole and the sweltering heat of the earth's deserts. They inhabit

Many of our most familiar birds come north to the U.S. and Canada only to breed, returning in autumn to the tropics. There they often find their native forests have been removed or burned, as in this scene from Ecuador.

fields and forests, mountains and valleys; some even spend all or most of their lives at sea.

Loss and Survival

Widespread awareness has been raised about the loss of habitat in Central and South America, places where many of the birds that breed in North America spend their winters. Closer to home, there is loss of habitat in our own neighborhoods and the land that surrounds us. Increasingly, many species return in spring to find that their breeding grounds have been bulldozed to make room for a strip mall or a housing development. Without the proper habitat, these birds cannot successfully nest and rear young. They cannot find adequate food supplies, and they are subjected to even greater threats from predators. Plants and insects that are intertwined with the life of a bird also face the same bleak outlook. As such, it is becoming increasingly important for us to preserve habitat wherever we can. A great place to start is by protecting or creating habitat in your own backyard. Plantings, feeders, water sources, and nesting provisions are just a few of the elements of habitat that will be covered in this book.

Natural Beauty

The addition of native plantings, nesting boxes, and water features not only helps birds but also enhances the natural beauty of your yard. Please note the term "natural beauty"; in this book we will discuss things that are attractive to birds, not to human beings. When it comes to creating a bird-friendly habitat, form must follow function. You will find no recommendations for artsy, ornate, and less-than-functional elements for your yard. When it comes to the birds, the more natural the better. Be aware that by creating attractive bird habitat you will also attract other forms of wildlife. Squirrels, groundhogs, opossums, skunks, raccoons, butterflies, dragonflies, and many other creatures will find your bird-friendly habitat inviting. Welcome them as part of the well-balanced ecosystem you are creating.

Variety is the secret to backyard habitats; any monoculture produces little variety. Even simple flower plantings should be varied, in this case by both open flowers for butterflies and insects (bird food) and tubular red flowers for hummingbirds.

An American Robin among berries. Backyard plants should be useful to the birds.

Chapter One

Evaluating Your Habitat

The simple mix of trees and shrubs that accompanies many typical backyards caters to the needs of chickadees, titmice, nuthatches, woodpeckers, and wrens, as well as a handful of other birds. But, that's generally where the list ends. This book is devoted to eliminating the monoculture of backyards and to planning for biodiversity. By doing so, you greatly increase the odds of attracting many other species that call your piece of property home.

Birds and Biodiversity

It is fairly safe to say that a well-manicured suburban lawn, with maybe a few shrubs and flowers, is not going to attract a great variety of birdlife. Basically, these yards are what biologists call a "monoculture."

What this means is that the habitat is biased toward one type of grass or shrub or tree. This does not promote "biodiversity," which is one of the key concepts of a successful backyard habitat. Biodiversity means that many species are well represented, catering to the needs of a much greater variety of life. In simple English, the needs of the birds are as varied as the species of birds that populate the world, each one fitting into a niche in its ecosystem. The more variety you provide in your habitat—in terms of trees, shrubs, flowers, and grasses—the more variety of birds you may attract.

GO NATIVE

Native plants, or those that are indigenous to your region, are best suited to providing your native birds with natural sources of food and shelter. Local nurseries and gardening experts can provide you with more information about using native plants in your habitat plan.

The Drawing Board

The first step in creating your very own backyard habitat is by taking a good look at your property and its existing features. Perhaps the easiest way to do so is to sit down with pencil and paper and make a diagram of your yard or outdoor space; keep in mind that this can be done for an urban outdoor patio, suburban backyard, or rural expanse of farmland. This will not only give you a great reference as to what's already there, but it will also show you where you have room to add.

A backyard habitat must be attractive to birds, not necessarily humans. Old trees, for instance, should be left standing to supply nesting areas for woodpeckers such as this Northern Flicker.

Firethorn, Pyracantha, *is a common backyard planting, but is it really attractive to your local birds? If not, replace it with holly, chokecherry, or small dogwoods that attract and hold birds.*

Take note of your trees (what are they, and do they serve wildlife?) and shrubs (are they purely ornamental, or would they be better suited for bird shelter if they were relocated?). Do any of your existing plantings produce seeds, nuts, or berries? Don't overlook flowers (do any provide nectar for hummingbirds?). What about water sources? Should you move that neglected birdbath to a more suitable location? Keep in mind any seasonal changes that occur in your backyard.

Once you have a clear idea of what there is to work with, make a list of any elements of habitat that might be missing or in need of enhancement. Perhaps you have several birdfeeders scattered throughout the yard, but none of them seem to attract much bird action; think about grouping them together as a feeding station or moving them to a different location. Consider which types of plantings are missing and where. Remember to look at the big picture. Your habitat will be complete only after you've provided all three elements: food, water, and shelter.

As you look at your property and think about its future, keep in mind that you'll probably want a good view of what is going on outside. Plan your plantings accordingly. Put the low shrubs, vines, and ground cover nearest your window and slowly build your way up to the tallest trees. This way, as you look out your window your eyes will naturally climb up through the various life zones you've planted.

As always, check with your local landscape professional to see which of the bird-friendly species discussed in this book will work best for you.

A male Broad-tailed Hummingbird feeding on nectar from Penstemon barbatus.

Chapter Two

Food for Thought

Nature's Bounty

When someone initially considers ways to attract birds to their yard, birdfeeding almost always is the first thing to spring to mind. Although birdfeeding is an excellent way to attract birds to your backyard sanctuary, it is technically artificial habitat enhancement. This book is dedicated to going beyond your birdfeeders and using nature to provide for the birds. In fact, the number of birds that regularly consume seed represents a mere fraction of the total population of birds in the United States. More than 900 species of birds have been identified in

North America, but only a handful of them will visit a birdfeeder. So how is it possible to see a greater variety of avian life? Aside from crisscrossing the country to find them, you can add new birds to your list by adding sources of nature's bounty to your yard.

Birds and plants go hand in hand. Birds rely on plants for so many different aspects of their daily lives. In fact, it's safe to say that the fewer plants around, the fewer the birds, too. Birds depend on plants for food, for shelter from storms, and for protection against predators. They build their nests and raise their young in the boughs of trees and the deep tangles of underbrush. The blossoms of many flowers attract hummingbirds and butterflies, adding even more color and wonder to the scene outside your window.

Although this chapter will cover birdfeeding and the types of seeds that can attract birds to your property, bear in mind that the best backyards are the ones that balance feeders with nature; in other words, use feeders as supplements and focal points, but let nature do the rest of the work. Birdfeeding is a lot of fun and can allow you to view some wondrous creatures up close and personal, but don't neglect the non-seedeating birds. You'll miss quite a parade.

Making Sense of Seeds

The quickest and easiest way to enhance your yard is to provide the birds with food, namely birdseed. Fortunately, many of the birds that actually live in and around backyards are seedeaters. According to U.S.

Many choices in birdseeds, from basic mixes to specialty blends, as well as bells and cakes, are available. Choose what is right for your yard and the birds you wish to attract. Photo courtesy of Kaytee® Products, Inc.

A gourmet seed mix will help you attract a wide variety of garden birds, from cardinals and finches to woodpeckers. Photo courtesy of Kaytee® Products, Inc.

government statistics, one out of four Americans feeds birds. It is commonly misunderstood that the process is as simple as buying a bag of "seed" and throwing it out to the birds. But in birdfeeding, as with most everything else, some research and a few basic principles can greatly enhance your experience.

The best place to start is with the seed itself. Unfortunately, not everything labeled "wild bird food" is really eaten by the birds. Much of the seed that we see in the supermarkets and stores is loaded with filler products that many birds simply aren't interested in. Being an educated consumer is the best way to approach birdfeeding. Read the list of ingredients on the bag of birdseed you are about to buy. Research has shown that black oil sunflower seed is the single most attractive seed you can offer your backyard guests. Northern Cardinals, grosbeaks, chickadees, titmice, and finches of all ilk readily consume this seed. Filler seeds such as milo, wheat, oats, rice, canary seed, cracked corn, and "mixed grain products" generally do nothing but add weight. The purpose of mixed birdseed should always be to increase the number of bird visits and the variety of birds visiting, not decrease cost. A good rule of thumb is not to purchase a mixed seed that is less expensive than pure black oil sunflower. This will mean, first of all, that black oil sunflower is not the primary ingredient and that "filler" seeds have been added to fill out the bag. A good mix may also include black stripe sunflower, peanut kernels (split peanuts or peanut halves), some white proso millet, sunflower chips (sunflower seeds without the shells), and perhaps some other nuts. These ingredients can attract species such as woodpeckers, nuthatches, and native sparrows.

Seed Choices

BLACK OIL SUNFLOWER

BLACK OIL SUNFLOWER: The cornerstone of a sound feeding program and the single most preferred seed you can offer. It should be the primary ingredient in any mixed birdseed. Cardinals, grosbeaks, chickadees, titmice, nuthatches, and finches all flock to this seed.

BLACK STRIPE SUNFLOWER: Although eaten by some of the larger birds such as Northern Cardinals and birds in the grosbeak family, black stripe is still not as readily eaten as black oil sunflower. It is more difficult for birds like chickadees, titmice, and nuthatches to open. This seed also has a lower meat-to-shell ratio than oilers, despite its larger size; it is generally more expensive.

BLACK STRIPE SUNFLOWER

PEANUT KERNELS: Perhaps the second most attractive food you can put out for birds. You can increase the number of visits from jays, woodpeckers, nuthatches, chickadees, titmice, and Northern Cardinals by offering peanuts kernels.

MILLET

WHITE PROSO MILLET: These small, pearly white seeds are most preferred by ground-feeding birds. Best served on a platform/fly-through feeder, slightly elevated ground feeder, or broadcast directly on the ground. Red-winged Blackbirds, as well as most sparrows, doves, juncos, towhees, and buntings, are attracted to millet.

Whole Peanuts: Due to their large size, whole peanuts must be offered in open feeders. Jays have been known to fly in from every direction upon hearing the sound of whole peanuts hitting the bottom of a feeder. Whole peanuts will also attract crows, magpies, titmice, and woodpeckers.

Safflower: What makes safflower a good addition to a feeding station is not what it attracts, but what it doesn't. Safflower is not attractive to grackles, European Starlings, and squirrels. This is an excellent seed to offer by itself, but it loses any of its value when offered in a mix. The visitors you are trying to discourage by using safflower will still come to the mix and either sweep away the safflower or just leave it there.

Safflower

Nyjer (Niger)

Nyjer (Thistle): Another seed to be offered on its own, in a specialized feeder designed for economical dispensing. This expensive seed is most attractive to American Goldfinches, redpolls, and Pine Siskins. Also spelled niger.

Corn: Although jays and some woodpeckers will often consume it, corn, especially the cracked variety, is primarily used as filler. In warm, wet weather, cracked corn has a tendency to mold rapidly. Use corn to feed your squirrels, not your birds.

Mixed Grain Products: May contain wheat, oats, rice, flax, milo, canary seed, etc. Although it makes a very inexpensive food offering, it makes for a very unattractive seed mix for most of the birds you are trying to attract.

Winter Wheat

Feeder Fashions

Feeders are the best way to offer food to your backyard residents. There are three basic designs: the tube feeder, usually made of plastic and designed to hang from a tree or hook; the simple platform feeder, which may or may not be covered; and the hopper feeder, basically a platform feeder with a Plexiglas center (hopper) to hold and dispense seed. Although some people have success just throwing seed on the ground, by doing so you are excluding some birds that won't feed down there. Also, birds that feed on the ground are much more at risk from predators than those that use feeders.

Tube feeders are generally designed to dispense black oil sunflower. The perching birds that visit these feeders have such a strong preference for sunflower that it rarely makes sense to offer mixes in them. If you have used mixes in a tube feeder, you've probably seen the birds employ a technique called "bill sweeping." They do this to rid the feeder of everything else as they dig for the black oil sunflower. This means you wind up losing a lot of seed to the ground and have to fill your feeder more often. Thistle feeders, used primarily to attract the American Goldfinch, are a special type of tube feeder with small ports to accommodate the small size of thistle (technically known as nyjer or niger) seed.

Of all feeder styles on the market, hopper feeders are probably the most popular. A good hopper feeder will attract a wide variety of birds—both perching and ground feeding—to its large landing area. Although it

Seed bells, basically a seed mix held together by suet, will attract many chickadees and titmice.

is unusual to see a Northern Cardinal, grosbeak, or jay land on a tube feeder (particularly without a tray), they will readily visit hopper feeders. Hopper feeders are also popular because of their carrying capacity; most hold several pounds of birdseed and don't have to be filled as often as tube feeders. Because of the variety of birds that will use it, a hopper feeder is an excellent place to feed a high-quality mix.

Covered platform feeders draw a great variety of birds because they can be used with foods of many sizes and types. This Red-bellied Woodpecker may be looking for peanuts.

The most attractive style of feeder to the highest number of species is the fly through (or covered platform). The open style of this feeder allows birds easy access to the food as well as the ability to leave quickly in whichever direction they choose. Because there is no dispensing system to clog, you can use this feeder for larger foods. Offer peanuts in the shell, for example, if you want regular visits from jays. You can also serve fruit; in warmer weather, try putting out grapes, blueberries, bananas, or oranges and watch for visits from catbirds, orioles, and tanagers. The most important feature of fly-through feeders is adequate drainage. Look for one with a screened bottom or with holes drilled in the base for water to escape.

Hulled sunflower seeds are expensive, but they prevent waste, are eaten by almost all backyard birds, and don't produce hull deposits on the ground, reducing cleanup time.

There are hundreds of feeder designs on the market today, not to mention the overwhelming number of food choices. The best place to start is to take a look at your backyard, see which birds already frequent it, check a field guide for what birds you can hope to attract, and *then* go shopping. A little knowledge can go a long way in helping you achieve success with your feeding project.

A small garden pond provides an attraction for many types of birds.

Chapter Three

Water, the Source of Life

If you can choose only one element to enhance your natural bird habitat, consider adding moving water. Although various birds are attracted to different trees, shrubs, vines, and fruit, virtually every bird is attracted to water. They all must drink and bathe, and they must do so all year long.

If your property already has a natural water source, you should first evaluate it for birds, not for other wildlife or its esthetic value. The water must be slow, shallow, and reliable. If you have a lake or river on your property, this may not help you attract many prospective backyard birds. Consider adding a water feature designed specifically for the birds.

Of all the elements you can add to a backyard habitat, water is by far the one that can yield the greatest diversity of birdlife. For example, a small recirculating pond can quickly and easily draw in a surprising variety of species. Add a mister that sprays down the leaves of nearby plants and then drips into the pond to further tempt the birds. Although it can take months, sometimes years, for habitat enhancements such as tree plantings to take hold and begin attracting birds, water may do it as soon as you walk away.

Birdbaths

The classic birdbath can be an effective way of providing water for bathing and drinking birds, provided that a few points are taken into consideration. First and foremost, the water must always be kept clean and fresh. Birds should not be forced to drink stagnant or dirty water. If you include a birdbath in your habitat plan, it is crucial that the water be changed daily; by doing so, maintenance should be fairly simple—unless a buildup of algae is allowed to occur. Handle algae with a stiff scrub brush and a mixture of equal parts hot water and white vinegar. If the birdbath is especially dirty, let the solution sit in the bath for an hour or two then scrub it out and rinse it well. Note that concrete baths may become stained green from algae. It may be impossible to remove all of the algae, but the bath should be fine as long as algae is not floating in the water.

A simple, easy to clean birdbath will attract birds of all types, including some that do not come to feeders. Here a male Northern Cardinal enjoys a sip.

Many commercial birdbaths actually are too deep for the birds. The maximum depth should be between 1 and 2 inches.

Depth is another important aspect of a birdbath. Too many of those on the market today are actually too deep for birds to use. Birds such as the American Robin require only between an inch and an inch and a half to bathe in; smaller birds like finches and kinglets require even less. If your birdbath is more than an inch and a half deep, try placing some flat rocks in the bath to offer varying depths, which should attract different birds. Birds are accustomed to drinking and bathing in the small trickles of water that slowly feed streams. This depth flaw is especially true of some of the more ornamental concrete birdbaths.

Although the concrete birdbath is the one that most consumers identify with, there are quite a few alternatives now on the market offering easier cleaning and more durability. The birdbath of today and beyond is either a cedar or metal frame that holds a shallow plastic bowl. The bowl is lightweight, easy to remove, and even easier to clean. Just remove the bowl and bring it inside to scrub or soak overnight. The new designs have addressed another problems associated with concrete birdbaths: cracking and wearing away over time. Replacement bowls can be difficult to find, and patching is not usually foolproof, so the consumer is then faced with buying an entirely new birdbath setup. The plastic basins available for the newer wood or steel baths are easily and inexpensively replaced.

CLEANING SOLUTION

Vinegar can be used to clean virtually all of your backyard bird accessories. Bleach and ammonia, even diluted, are caustic and could eventually cause discoloration and deterioration of your feeders and birdbaths.

Pottery and terra-cotta birdbaths have their own advantages and disadvantages. Although pleasing to the eye, they offer little durability and can crack very easily. Their stands or pedestals also tend to be more unstable than other designs, making them less attractive to birds. Because most birds prefer a stable base for bathing, hanging birdbaths may also be avoided. Birds will occasionally visit them, but they are accustomed to finding water on the ground, in puddles, small slow streams, and the like. When creating a bird-friendly and natural habitat, your goal is to maximize your property's attractiveness to birds. By placing your water feature on or near the ground, your results will be much greater.

Wintertime and Water

Many people retire their birdbaths the minute colder weather sets in each year. This is not advisable, as birds require water for drinking and bathing throughout the year. The water sources that remain available during the cold of winter are typically either moving too fast or are too deep for birds to use. For this reason, birdbath deicers are the accepted way to make sure your birds have the ability to find water when needed, despite freezing temperatures.

THE BIG CHILL

Yes, birds do need to bathe in the wintertime, even when the temperature seems far too cold. Bathing helps birds keep their feathers clean, which is essential for proper insulation. Dirty feathers mean cold spots; cold spots mean loss of precious body heat. All living creatures need to drink, no matter what the weather, birds even more so, for each time they exhale they are losing moisture from their bodies.

Deicers come in many styles, shapes, and designs. One of the most desirable features in deicers is that they are thermostatically controlled, meaning they only operate when the temperatures warrant, and they automatically shut down during warmer spells. They also shut off if they should happen to fall out of a birdbath; some models turn themselves off after being out of the water for about five minutes. Deicers also come in a wide array of power strengths. Which deicer you need depends on what you're trying to keep ice-free. Look for a good, durable design and one that carries a three- or four-year warranty. At this time, solar-powered birdbath deicers are not available, most likely due to the size and cost of the solar panel that would be needed to keep a water feature open.

Drippers and Misters

Relatively new additions to the world of birdbaths are "drippers" and "misters," which do exactly what their names imply. When added to a good birdbath, drippers and misters can increase bird traffic for a very modest investment. These accessories connect to your outdoor water source via a length of rubber tubing and a Y valve, allowing the simultaneous use of your garden hose and water feature. The flow rates are regulated by needle valves. Ideally, you should dig a small trench in the ground with an edging tool and bury your line to avoid running over it with the lawn mower or having other backyard visitors (chipmunks are notorious for this) chew holes in the tubing.

Drippers are placed in or next to a birdbath and provide a slow but steady drip into the basin. The movement of the water is very attractive to birds. Some, such as chickadees and titmice, have been known to land right on the tip of the dripper tube and drink straight from it. (Bird photographers have long known of the value of a dripper in their field photography, often setting up a dripper to entice otherwise shy birds within the reach of their lenses.) Drippers are also labor-saving devices because the steady supply of water does a great job of keeping your birdbath full and fresh; if it should need refilling, simply open the needle valve wide and your dripper will flow like a hose, quickly filling your bath.

Birds are well-adapted to survive through normal winters and need little special attention except during extended periods of cold and ice. If you can keep a birdbath free of ice, however, the birds will appreciate it.

Misters are another birdbath accessory that runs off your outdoor water faucet. However, instead of slowly dripping water into your birdbath, misters create a fine mist over and around your bath. There are two basic mister styles. The first sits in the birdbath itself and shoots the mist straight up. This version is most effective when there is a great deal of shrubbery around your bath. The mist will gather on the leaves and drip down into your bath; the wet leaves can be seen from a distance by birds and will announce that water is available. These misters are especially attractive to hummingbirds, which have even been spotted flying through lawn sprinklers on warm summer days.

Black-capped Chickadees can survive very bad winters, but they still need to bathe to keep their feathers clean.

The other style of mister, the leaf mister, is put directly in a shrub or tree near a birdbath or other water feature. This product is designed first and foremost to encourage leaf bathing and then to drip some water into your bath. A great number of birds will frequent leaf misters: chickadees, titmice, Northern Cardinals, goldfinches, and many of the warblers.

Bird Ponds

As the hobby of birdfeeding and habitat enhancement has grown, the diversity of backyard bird ponds has increased by leaps and bounds, allowing almost anyone to add moving water to their yard with only as much work as they are willing to undertake. More and more habitat enthusiasts are adding these liquid bird magnets to their yards with amazing results. Keep in mind, however, that bird ponds should not be confused with water gardens or ornamental fishponds. The specifications of bird ponds must be designed to meet the unique requirements of birds.

A standard bird pond requires a shallow hole lined with some kind of watertight liner. The size of a pond can vary, but 3 feet by 5 feet is an average size. Because most ponds have a waterfall or some other feature that requires a pump to keep the water moving, the chosen site must be within easy reach of an electrical outlet.

Pick a level area of your yard and mark off the shape and location of the pond with some stakes. Then grab your shovel and start digging. Your pond needs to be dug deep in the middle and shallow at the edges. In doing so, the birds will be able to wade gradually in to whatever depth they please. Again, optimal depth for most bird bathing is only approximately an inch and a half. The deeper center is necessary for your recirculating pump. You can use rocks to create the proper depths as well as hide the pump from view; these rocks will also give your pond a very natural look.

Along with providing excellent stepping points for the birds, the small rocks will act as a filtration system, keeping a great deal of larger debris from clogging your pump. Please note that backyard ponds require a great deal of maintenance. Ponds and their pumps require regular cleaning of the mud, leaves, twigs, pebbles, and

MISTERS AND DRIPPERS: COMMON QUESTIONS

Should misters and drippers be left on all day? No. Turn them on only when you want to watch the birds bathe. Alternatively, you could use one of the computerized watering timers to turn your drippers and misters on and off automatically. If you do this, or turn your water on at about the same time each day, the birds will become accustomed to the schedule and show up for their daily shower.

How much water do misters and drippers use? Drippers use markedly less water than misters. You can regulate the rate to a drip every second or two, which will consume about a pint or so an hour. A mister, with the needle regulating valve wide open, can use about three gallons an hour. Turning the valve down can lower the water consumption rate to about a gallon an hour; most misters stop misting below this rate. Obviously, you should check local water regulations before using these devices.

A simple plastic-lined pond with a fountain or waterfall is easy to construct and maintain and relatively inexpensive.

In the northeastern U.S., Canada Geese may become a nuisance at even small ponds. They seem to be especially attracted to ponds in larger lawns and fields where they also can feed on low grasses.

bird droppings that accumulate and can cause the mechanics of your pump to seize up. If you put in a pond, be prepared to occasionally get wet and/or dirty. If you are looking for low maintenance water features, stick with a birdbath and mister or dripper.

Add levels and cascades to your pond as you see fit. Your pond can be everything from a puddle with a pump to a miniature river emptying into a small lake. Just remember that white-water rapids are not going to attract birds in the long run (although birds will be attracted to any sounds of running or dripping water). Instead, design any cascades and waterfalls so they fall gently. A nice meandering, shallow stream flowing into a small, shallow pond should be your goal.

Adding a mister or dripper to the pond can help keep it full and fresh, as well as attract additional birdlife. Position a mister so that it sprays into the surrounding foliage to wet down the leaves and drip down into the pond basin itself. You will be surprised at the terrific job it does of keeping your pond topped off, catering to those birds that prefer to leaf-bathe rather than dunk themselves.

You can maintain your pond all year long by adding a deicing device. Look for one that is designed with ponds in mind, because some of the lower powered models designed for birdbaths won't be strong enough for your mini river and lake system. With a pond deicer, there's no need to worry about the auto shut-off feature. Just bury the deicer down in the small rocks at the bottom of the pond and enjoy! Watching birds flock to open water in the dead of winter is quite a treat.

BATHING BEAUTIES

Of the recent additions to the pond/birdbath portfolio of products for bird lovers, perhaps the most popular is the aboveground pond, a prefabricated plastic basin that provides enough water to recirculate but is not too deep for the birds to use. Their only requirements are a flat area and a source of electricity. Place the "pond" on the ground, fill it up, plug it in, and it's ready to go. In time, your native plants will grow up around the pond and give it a natural look. These ponds can also be enhanced with drippers, misters, and some small flat rocks to allow smaller birds access.

Some very clever new designs in natural-looking birdbaths have also started to appear on the market. Baths that replicate a sassafras tree stump or a boulder, both made of cast resin and weighing far less than the real thing, can be purchased with drippers built right in. There are also ground-level birdbaths, basically miniature prefabricated ponds that either have built-in drippers or have the option of including a very low-flow waterfall. For those bird-lovers looking for something different from the classic birdbath design, these new choices may be the solution.

FIGHTING SLIME

Algal growth is one of the major drawbacks of a bird pond. However, floating plants or bog plants, which grow with their roots underwater, actually inhibit algal growth. Many nurseries carry a selection of these specialty plants, not only to keep your pond algae-free, but to add to the natural esthetics of your pond. Plants that would fit this description include Blue Flag, Water Mint, Water Celery, New Guinea Impatiens, Yellow Water Iris, Cardinal Flower, Watercress, Water Pennywort, Dwarf Umbrella Palm, Four Leaf Water Clover, and some small varieties of hostas. As always, check with your local nursery for the plants that will work best in your area.

A heavily planted pond such as this is not really necessary to attract birds all year. Large, complicated ponds require much more maintenance than smaller ponds and thus tend to be more expensive to keep.

Nesting boxes often attract Tree Swallows, colorful birds that help control insect nuisances.

Chapter Four

Providing Shelter

Nesting Boxes

Another way to enhance your backyard habitat is to add shelter, typically in the form of several nesting boxes. Please notice that they are not being referred to as "birdhouses" in this book. Birds don't actually live in these structures. Cavity-nesting birds generally build their nest (in some cases, they don't build anything at all) in the box, raise their young, fledge them, and then are done with the box. For most of North America's cavity-nesters, the whole process, from egg-laying to fledging, takes approximately one month.

The term "cavity-nester" is applied to the group of birds that do not build their nests out in the open.

Woodpeckers (here a Red-headed Woodpecker) excavate nest holes in living and dead trees; their abandoned nests often are used by many other small birds as well.

Usually the nest structures built by these birds are so flimsy that they require the sides and walls of a box (or natural tree cavity) to hold them together. Woodpeckers don't build any nest at all, but lay their eggs in the remnant wood chips left over from nest-hole excavation.

What did the birds do before nest boxes? Well, before nest boxes there were a great deal of dead and dying trees around. These provided perfect opportunities for woodpeckers to excavate cavities that in subsequent years would be used by a second round of cavity-nesters. However, as suburbia and development have spread, dead or dying tress have been removed, sometimes the minute they show any inclination of ill health. Unfortunately, this is not a prudent approach to habitat maintenance. There is often more life going on in a tree that is dead or dying than in one that is still fully green. Many creatures require trees in this state for their shelter and their food. When we remove these trees, we are effectively removing an essential piece of habitat for many creatures, including birds, insects, and mammals.

Nesting boxes work well with birds that place their nests in holes in old trees, the cavity-nesters. Here a Carolina Chickadee looks out of its nest box. Notice that the opening is not much larger than the diameter of the bird, restricting usage of the nest to just a few small species.

In other cases, certain trees, especially apple trees, create natural cavities of their own. The Eastern Bluebird was at its highest numbers when apple trees were left to their own devices. Since the advent of industrial farming and the removal of many suitable nesting sites, the bluebirds (Eastern, Western, and Mountain) have all come to rely on man's help. Bluebird trails have been erected across the country to help these lovely creatures survive and thrive in a world that has all but eliminated its natural habitat. It is through these efforts that our bluebirds have made an astounding comeback and should be with us for generations to come.

Building for Bluebirds

If you'd like to establish bluebirds on your property, it is important to note that it is a fairly labor-intensive project. Because bluebirds have come to rely on our efforts to help re-establish them in their habitat, it is important to do so responsibly.

The location of bluebird boxes is extremely important. Bluebird boxes generally do better when mounted on posts in open fields off the edge of a wooded area. Boxes mounted on trees are much more likely to either be taken over by competing species (House or Carolina Wrens, chickadees, etc.) or be raided by raccoons, snakes, or other predators.

You should start a logbook and keep track of the progress of the nesting. Note the date that nest building starts and, most importantly, the day the eggs are laid and the day the eggs hatch. After the eggs hatch you should make sure that the young are doing well and are not being parasitized by blowfly larvae. If they are, dispose of the infested nest and replace it with a new nest made out of some dried grasses (parent birds will not abandon a nest due to human contact). Twelve days after hatching you should stop your box inspections. Any disturbance from this point on could cause premature fledging of the young, which are due to leave within the next two to ten days.

Due to the amount of monitoring required, you should erect your bluebird box or boxes at an easily accessible height. Five and a half to six feet off the ground will usually suffice and allow you sufficient room to install a predator guard if needed.

Man helped reduce Eastern Bluebird populations by introducing European Starlings to this country, and now manmade nesting boxes on bluebird trails are helping the birds recover.

Nesting boxes are a great way of enticing birds to take advantage of your backyard hospitality. Keep a record of the birds that nest in your yard, when they set up housekeeping, and when the youngsters fledge, year after year. It will be a wonderful addition to your backyard birding experience.

Construction 101

There are certain aspects of nest box construction that are noteworthy. Boxes are best left undecorated; remember that you are trying to replicate a natural tree cavity. Certain paints and stains also may have a toxic effect on birds and nestlings. The wood of choice is either cedar or kiln-dried white pine, as these two will last the longest when exposed to the elements. Plywood, due to its chemical binders, should never be used in the construction of nesting boxes. In fact, any treated wood should be avoided.

Look for nesting boxes or plans that are designed with birds in mind. The proper size entrance holes, the proper size floors, and the correct distance from the hole to the floor are all facets in making up a good nesting box.

Perches are an open invitation to nest predators and should never be included in a nest box. The birds that use nesting boxes have claws adapted to clinging to wood. This is yet another reason why the wood should be raw and untreated. It makes access easier for those that belong in the box. Some nesting boxes are even designed with a built-in predator guard, which is an extra piece of wood attached to the front of the box, effectively doubling the depth of the wood around the entrance hole. This prevents any predator from sticking its head or claws in deep enough to reach the nestlings or eggs at the bottom of the box.

If the bluebird boxes mentioned earlier sound like too much work, take heart. There are plenty of other species that use nesting boxes that require virtually no maintenance. Wrens, chickadees, titmice, nuthatches, woodpeckers, swallows, Great Crested Flycatchers, and even an owl or two will use nesting boxes. Non-cavity-nesting birds such as the American Robin, Barn Swallow, and Eastern Phoebe will avail themselves of nesting platforms (basically a shelf onto which they can build a nest) that can be put up much like boxes. Below is a chart that will give you some basic dimensions for proper nesting boxes if you should decide to build your own.

Keep nest boxes simple. Elaborate construction, decorative accents, perches, and bright colors all tend to cause problems for potential occupants. Natural finishes and ease of cleaning are your main requirements in a nest box.

NESTING BOX DIMENSIONS

Birds	Mounting Height (feet)	House Height (inches)	Entrance Hole (inches)	Distance from hole to floor	Floor Size (inches)
Chickadees	4-8	10	1.12-1.25	8 inches	4x4
Titmice	4-12	10	1.25	8 inches	4x4
Carolina Wren*	4-8	8	1.25-1.5	6 inches	4x4
House Wren*	Almost anywhere	6-8	1-1.25	6 inches	4x4
Downy Woodpecker	8-12	10-12	1.25-1.5	8 inches	4x4 with shaving left in
Red-bellied Woodpecker	8-15	15	2	10-12 inches	6x6
Red-headed Woodpecker	8-15	15	2	10-12 inches	6x6
Eastern Bluebird	5-7	8	1.5	6 inches	5x5
Nuthatches	8-15	8-10	1.25	6 inches	4x4
Northern Flicker	8-15	18	2.5	14 inches	7x7
Tree Swallow	5-7	8	1.5	6 inches	5x5
Screech Owls	15-20	15	3	10-12 inches	8x8

*It is worth noting that for wren boxes an oval hole (width-wise) may help out the birds who build their nests of thousands of little twigs, the wider opening facilitating this time-consuming process.

European Starlings have helped reduce numbers of larger cavity-nesting birds such as the bluebirds by aggressively taking over suitable nesting spots. For this reason most bird-friendly habitats tend to have few starlings.

Nesting Box Problems

Invaders

Sometimes, no matter how hard we try, we are not always able to attract the right birds to our nest boxes. To begin, boxes with entrance holes bigger than an inch and a half will likely end up housing the European Starling, a common and unwelcome interloper. Starlings are very aggressive and very prolific cavity-nesters, inhabiting almost every vacant hole they can find. If you find European Starlings beginning to build a nest in your box, remove the nesting material and continue to do so until they get the hint.

Another overly aggressive cavity-nester that should be deterred from nesting in your boxes is the House Sparrow. These birds are much smaller than European Starlings and can get into even smaller boxes. Like the starlings, they should be discouraged from nesting by your consistent removal of their ungainly, messy nest of assorted nest materials.

Please note that both the European Starling and the House Sparrow are not native species to North America and are therefore not afforded the protection of all other bird species. *However, It is not permitted to disturb any other birds nesting in any way to prevent them from using a nesting box.* It is therefore critical that you be able to identify the birds in your yard and those that are using your nesting boxes before you haphazardly remove the nest of a bird.

Predators

The other issue to deal with is predation by raccoons, snakes, and even other birds. By placing your nesting box on a pole, with a metal predator guard underneath it (also known as a squirrel baffle when placed under a birdfeeder), you can effectively eliminate the threat of raccoons or snakes invading your nesting boxes. If your nesting boxes are mounted on trees, preventing these predators is all but impossible. Unfortunately, a great many cavity-nesting birds prefer their boxes mounted on trees, hardwood trees (oaks, maples, etc.) to be precise.

Predation by other birds such as jays or crows can be remedied by either purchasing a box with a predator guard or installing one yourself. To install one yourself, simply mount a block of wood over the nest box entrance hole and redrill the correct size through the block and into the box. It creates an entrance "tunnel" that is too long for these birds to reach through to get to the bottom of the nesting box.

Squirrels of all types are nuisances at the feeder, smelling seeds even in empty feeders. They can climb almost anything and will destroy feeders to get into them, chewing through wood and plastics. Many keepers provide separate feeders for squirrels and learn to enjoy their antics.

Plants attract insects, and insects attract birds. These zinnias are both colorful and bird-friendly.

Chapter Five

Planting to Attract Birds

Part of the American culture is to have a well-manicured swath of green surrounding our homes; unfortunately, this kind of monoculture is anathema to nature. Nature is diverse; it requires many different elements to thrive. One way to achieve this diversity is to return your little patch of earth to its former, untended splendor. If you lack the patience to wait for nature to do the planting for you, there are many ways you can help things along. The most obvious of these is to plant shrubs, vines, and trees that are beneficial to birds and other wildlife. Again, a local nursery can be of great assistance. It is also important to research your climate and soil conditions to see which plantings will benefit your habitat most.

PUTTING DOWN ROOTS

Whether it be as a food source, as protection from weather and predators, or to provide safe nesting sites, trees, shrubs, and flowers all play an integral role in the creation of your bird-friendly habitat. Many of the shrubs and trees listed flower once a season, then provide fruit for birds. The handful of suggested plantings given here are native to this country and may have great value to your backyard habitat. Although not all of these specific species will be found nationwide, you should be able to find relatives that will thrive in your climate.

It is also becoming increasingly important that the majority, if not all, of your plantings be native plants, plants that are a normal part of your ecosystem. Although many imported or naturalized plants have great benefits for wildlife, birds especially, these plants may take over and become invasive, crowding out less aggressive native plants. Whether it be Multiflora Rose or Russian Olive, when birds eat the fruits from these introduced species they do not digest the seeds. As the birds fly and defecate, the undigested seeds fall to the ground and take root. Once started, many of these can take over a landscape, choking out other vegetation, thereby only favoring the birds and wildlife that benefit from that specific plant species. If you do plant any imported or naturalized plants, please take great care to keep them in check and not let them overwhelm your habitat. If you do have invasive species in your yard, remove them and replace them with native plants. The long-term benefits to you, your yard, and the wildlife that live there far outweigh any short-term losses.

Before we discuss what to plant to attract birds and other wildlife, it is important to note that the use of pesticides on and around any plants is to be avoided at all costs. These plants are providing food, and ingesting even the smallest amount of these chemicals can prove fatal to wildlife.

If possible, try to use mostly native plants in your backyard. Jewelweed is an excellent and colorful choice for the northeastern U.S. and also an effective antidote for stinging nettle rashes. Native plants usually require less care than foreign species, may use less water, are more insect-resistant, and tend not to cause a nuisance if they should escape.

Vines

American Bittersweet (*Ampelopsis cordata*): Great fruit provider, but be certain you are planting the *American* Bittersweet. There are Asian species that are to be avoided due to their invasive tendencies.

Honeysuckle (*Lonicera* species): An excellent source of nectar and cover for small songbirds. This is yet another plant that has Asian species that you should avoid.

Native honeysuckles are great plantings, with a variety of species for each region of North America. Coral Honeysuckle, Lonicera sempervirens, *also is very colorful and easy to grow.*

Trumpet Vine (*Campsis radicans*): The penultimate hummingbird attraction. If hummingbirds are in your area, this is one vine that will bring them to your yard. Like many other vines, it is a very strong grower. To keep tabs on it, run it up a trellis.

Wild grape (*Vitis* species): What Trumpet Vine is to hummingbirds, wild grape is to orioles, tanagers, catbirds, and more than 100 other bird species. It is also a terrific source of cover.

Large Shrubs and Small Trees

Serviceberry (*Amelanchier canadensis*): Grows between 5 and 25 feet in height and 8 to 10 feet in width. It will do best in moist, well-drained areas. It produces white flowers in the spring and is an important berry-bearing plant during the early summer. Bluebirds, robins, tanagers, and cardinals favor its berries.

Red Chokeberry (*Aronia arbutifolia*): This shrub grows to about 10 feet in height and 3 to 5 feet in width. It prefers full sun to partial shade and is adaptable to many types of soil. It also produces a white flower in late spring. Chickadees, titmice, and waxwings, as well as many other birds, eat the berries of this tree.

Common Chokecherry (*Prunus virginiana*): More than 40 species of birds have been known to visit this small tree for its clusters of red fruits. It can grow anywhere from 6 to 30 feet and does well in full sun. Cedar Waxwings are particularly fond of this fruit.

Red-osier Dogwood (*Cornus sericea*): This is a loose, broad shrub that grows 7 to 9 feet in height and 8 to 10 feet in circumference. It will thrive in a vast majority of soil types. It produces a white berry in the late summer that cardinals, grosbeaks, waxwings, vireos, and robins and other members of the thrush family thrive on.

Flowering Dogwood produces red fruits that are attractive to many birds over winter. The showy flowers also attract many insects in the spring and summer.

Flowering Dogwood (*Cornus florida*): This small tree (15 to 20 feet maximum) produces a red berry that is held through fall and winter and that is feasted upon by a large variety of birds, including grosbeaks, cardinals, and waxwings.

Mountain Dogwood (*Cornus nuttallii*): This hardy tree can grow to approximately 30 to 40 feet. It produces a fruit crop in clusters every fall. These berries can attract waxwings, woodpeckers, finches, and vireos.

Winterberry (*Ilex verticillata*): This type of deciduous holly requires both male and female plants to create berries. It grows to about 10 feet in height and can be almost as wide. The red berries are held into the winter and are an invaluable food source for mockingbirds, catbirds, thrashers, bluebirds, waxwings, and robins and other thrushes.

Mountain Laurel (*Kalmia laifolia*): A big, thick evergreen shrub that grows to 15 feet high and can provide a wonderful shelter for many birds and other backyard residents. It produces light pink flowers in the early summer. Deer are also quite fond of this.

Northern Bayberry (*Myrica pensylvanica*): An extremely adaptable shrub that does well in virtually any soil. Its fruit is eaten by a variety of birds and is especially relished by Yellow-rumped Warblers and Tree Swallows.

Fragrant Sumac (*Rhus aromatica*): Growing anywhere from 3 to 6 feet in height and 5 to 10 feet in girth, the Fragrant Sumac is a shrub that can thrive in many different soils. Another important source of winter food for many of our backyard birds. Bluebirds, American Robins and other thrushes, as well as Northern Cardinal and Northern Mockingbird count on this shrub's bounty to make it through rough winters.

High Bush Blueberry (*Vaccinum corymbossum*): This shrub can grow up to 12 feet in both directions and produces berries in the summer. It can attract tanagers, orioles, bluebirds, and robins and other thrushes.

Small Trees

Washington Hawthorn (*Crataegus phaenopyrum*): This small thorny tree grows up to about 30 feet in height and about the same in circumference. It produces a red berry that will last well into winter. Waxwings and native sparrows are particularly fond of this fruit, and the tree's built-in armor of thorns provides excellent nest site protection.

Red Mulberry (*Morus rubra*): When it comes to attracting birds, there are few species of plant to rival the mulberry. Its succulent fruits are devoured by orioles, cuckoos, tanagers, and many other species. It is often necessary when dealing with mulberry to make sure you have both male and female plants to produce berries. Be forewarned that birds make quite a mess with this fruit.

American Holly (*Ilex opaca*): Can grow up to 25 feet in height as well as 20 feet across. As with all holly, both male and female plants are necessary to produce berries. It bears a red berry, especially favored by thrashers and thrushes, throughout the fall and winter. Its sharply pointed leaves provide great nest security for many birds.

Mountain Ash (*Sorbus americana*): May reach heights exceeding 30 feet. It produces an orange-red berry late in the summer and holds it well into fall and early winter. These berries are readily eaten by Gray Catbirds, American Robins, bluebirds, waxwings, and others.

THE VIBURNUM FAMILY

Virtually all of these hardy plants serve birds well. They are attractive food and cover sources for Brown Thrashers, waxwings, Northern Mockingbirds, and American Robins and other thrushes. Check with your local nursery for the one best suited to your area.

American or Highbush Cranberrybush
(*Viburnum trilobum*)
Arrowwood Viburnum
(*Viburnum dentatum*)
Blackhaw Viburnum
(*Viburnum prunifolium*)
Mapleleaf Viburnum
(*Viburnum acerfolium*)
Nannyberry
(*Viburnum lentago*)

A couple of plants of Arrowwood Viburnum will provide cover for small birds; the purple fruits are eaten by many birds in the autumn and winter.

Hummingbirds and Your Garden

Hummingbirds are one of nature's most miraculous, fascinating, and sought-after creatures. The desert of southeastern Arizona boasts the largest number of different species of hummingbirds, including those that sometimes cross the border from Mexico. If you live in the East, however, you will find one species, the Ruby-throated Hummingbird, 99 percent of the time. These winged wonders frequent backyards across the country at different times of year. On the East Coast, hummingbird season usually is mid-spring into early fall; on the West Coast hummingbirds can be attracted all year long.

Black-chinned Hummingbird

The first and easiest way to attract hummingbirds to your yard is to put out a hummingbird feeder. In nature hummingbirds feed on flower nectar, so these feeders are designed to dispense a similar solution of sugar and water. It is a simple matter to make it yourself using the preferred ratio of four parts water to one part sugar. Bring the water to a boil, add the sugar, and bring it back to a boil for three or four minutes to allow the sugar to fully dissolve. Do not use honey, artificial sweeteners, sugar syrups, or anything else, just plain table sugar. Also, you should *not* add food coloring to your hummingbird nectar. If you could "milk" a flower, you would see a clear nectar, not red. In fact, when it comes to adding anything chemical to bird food of any kind, it is best to avoid doing so.

It is most important to keep your solution fresh (although extra juice can be stored in the refrigerator for up to about two weeks). In the heat of the summer, nectar can sour outside in just one day, causing harm to the hummingbirds. In fact, during the hottest spells of the year you may decide not to use the nectar feeders at all; instead just allow the hummingbirds to visit the plantings in your yard. Hummingbirds are perfectly capable of surviving in the wild, and they do not count on your feeder as their sole source of nutrition. Hummingbirds glean tiny insects from inside the flowers they feed from, and they are even quite adept at catching insects in mid-air.

Nesting Ruby-throated Hummingbird

A feeder is no guarantee that you will attract hummingbirds. The presence of the proper plants in your yard can go a long way to increasing the likelihood and number of hummingbird visitors. Both perennials and annuals can attract hummingbirds; many garden centers offer a wide selection of plants that require very little maintenance.

Hardy Fuchsia

Of all the plants you can add to your yard to attract hummingbirds, the Trumpet Vine (*Campsis radicans*) is perhaps the champion. Although it can take a couple of years to become established and bloom, once it does it grows rapidly and offers large red or red-orange trumpet-shaped blooms for birds. When planting Trumpet Vine, plan to train it to grow up an arbor or trellis, because once it gets a foothold, it is a strong, fast-growing vine that can easily take over.

There are dozens of flowers and plantings that will tempt hummingbirds. Some of them can be planted in hanging containers, some have to be planted in the ground, and others grow wild. One of the most attractive plants that grows naturally in many areas is the Spotted Jewelweed (*Impatiens capensis* or *Impatiens pallida*). Unlike many of the hummingbird plants, these flowers are neither tubular nor red, but it is a wonderful plant to have around your yard. If you happen to brush up against Poison Ivy, simply break off a piece of Jewelweed and rub the juice from the stem on the affected area to relieve the itching.

Other plants that can add to the attractiveness of your yard for hummingbirds include Bee Balm (*Monarda didyma*), Bleeding Heart (*Dicentra spectabilis*), Butterfly Bush (*Buddleia davidii*), Canada Columbine (*Aquilegia canadensis*), Cardinal Flower (*Lobelia cardinalis*), Carpet Bugle (*Ajuga reptans*), Coral Bells (*Heuchera sanguinea*), Dahlia (*Dahlia merckii*), Flowering Tobacco (*Nicotiana alata*), Four O'clock (*Mirabilis jalapa*), Fuchsia (*Fuchsia* species), hibiscus (*Hibiscus* species), hollyhocks (*Althea* species), Nasturtium (*Tropaeolum majus*), Larkspur (*Consolida ambigua*), penstemons (*Penstemon* species), petunias (*Petunia* species), Red Hot Poker (*Kniphofia uvaria*), Scarlet Sage (*Salvia splendens*), Sweet William (*Dianthus barbatus*), Zinnia (*Zinnia* species).

Shrubs and trees such as Azalea, Flowering Currant, Flowering Quince, Mimosa, and Flowering Crab can also lure in hummingbirds as well as add to the diversity of your bird garden.

Coral Honeysuckle

Large Trees

Common Hackberry (*Celtis occidentalis*): A large tree, growing up to and over 60 feet in height. Particularly hardy, thriving in most any conditions. The hackberry's fruit ranges in color from orange to purple and is relished by many songbirds, including the Cedar Waxwing, American Robin, Northern Mockingbird, and Eastern Bluebird.

Black Walnut is too large for many yards and produces quite a cleanup problem in the autumn, but its nuts are great for squirrels and woodpeckers.

Black Walnut (*Juglans nigra*): Grows up to 75 feet, producing chemicals that are toxic to other plants, which may give it a leg up on surrounding trees, but can be a nuisance for gardeners. Check with your nurseryman or local tree specialist to see how it will fit into your ecosystem. The nuts are eaten by many species of woodpecker.

White Pine (*Pinus strobus*): A fast-growing, very tall tree (up to 80 feet) that prefers well-drained soil. It is important to birds as a source of cover for nesting and escaping from predators. Its needles are commonly found in many bird nests, and its seeds are eaten by chickadees, titmice, nuthatches, and woodpeckers. If you do not have evergreen (coniferous) trees in your yard, this is an excellent starter tree due to its rapid growth and popularity with the birds. On any given evening many birds can be found roosting within its protective branches, either sleeping or just waiting out some inclement weather.

Oaks can provide not only cover but an excellent food source in the form of acorns, attractive to many large and small birds as well as squirrels.

Black Gum (*Nyssa sylvatica*): This tree can reach up to 50 feet in height and prefers soil that is well drained and acidic. It provides a dark blue fruit each autumn that is readily taken by many species of bird, including American Robins, Northern Flickers, thrashers, and mockingbirds, as well as many species of woodpecker.

Sycamore (*Platanus occidentalis*): A towering tree reaching heights well over 100 feet. Requires deep, moist, rich soils. The Sycamore is not terribly at home in most backyards. Its hanging seed balls are consumed by House Finches, Purple Finches, American Goldfinches, and Pine Siskins.

California Live Oak (*Quercus agrifolia*): A hardy species that can grow up to 75 feet tall. Produces acorns each fall. It is known to attract California Quail, Steller's Jays, chickadees, titmice, and many varieties of woodpeckers.

Giant Arborvitae (*Thuja plicata*): This tree can take up to 70 years to produce fruit, but, if you live on the Pacific Coast and it is in your yard, you should definitely leave it standing. It produces a massive seed crop approximately every third year and is attractive to many species of bird, including thrushes, nuthatches, and grosbeaks.

White Oak (*Quercus alba*): Can reach 100 feet in height. The White Oak is perhaps one of the most valuable trees to birdlife. Acorns are the preferred natural food for jays, nuthatches, woodpeckers, some thrushes, as well as many of the furred residents of your yard. A good crop of acorns can go a long way to ensuring a successful winter for wildlife.

Pines of all sorts are fast-growing, often very large trees that provide year-round cover, nesting habitat, and food for a variety of birds.

Bird-friendly Flowers

What's a bird-friendly habitat without the beautiful colors provided by flowers? Many of the flowers listed below can serve double duty in your yard as well. The seeds of these plants serve to attract the birds, and the blooms can attract butterflies, the other winged marvels of your backyard habitat.

Asters (*Aster* species): Flowers attract butterflies, provide seeds for birds

Bachelor's Buttons (*Centaurea hirta*): Seed provider

Basket Flower (*Centaurea americana*): Seed provider

Black-eyed Susan (*Rudbeckia* species): Seed provider, especially attractive to goldfinches

Calendula (*Calendula officinalis*): Seed provider

California Poppy (*Eschscholzia californica*): Seed provider

China Aster (*Callistephus chinensis*): Seed provider

Chrysanthemum (*Chrysanthemum* species): Seed provider

Coreopsis (*Coreopsis* species): Seed provider, blooms attract butterflies

Cornflower (*Centaurea cyanus*): Seed provider

Cosmos (*Cosmos* species): Seed provider

Goldenrod (*Solidago* species): Provides excellent cover after flower goes to seed, blooms attract butterflies

Globe thistle (*Echinops* species): Seed provider, also provides nesting material for American Goldfinch

Sunflowers (*Helianthus annuus*): Provides seeds to many birds

Zinnia (*Zinnia elegans*): Seed provider, blooms also attract butterflies

Although this list is by no means complete, these plantings can give your yard a lot of color and beauty as well as be attractive to a great many birds. As these flowers die, let them do so on their own and leave them through the fall. They will provide food and cover during the coming winter months. As with any and all plantings it is always best to consult a gardening professional who can properly advise as to what will thrive in your yard.

A bed of coneflowers (center) and other colorful plants will draw butterflies and other insects as well as producing seeds for finches. Scarlet or Texas Sage, Salvia coccinea, *has bright red tubular flowers (top) that are especially attractive to hummingbirds, which associate the color and form with nectar. A bed of sage is sure to draw the attention of migrating and perhaps nesting hummers. Sunflowers (bottom) are among the easiest plants to grow, but they are colorful and produce an important seed crop.*

Bringing in Butterflies

As more and more people become interested in the wildlife around them, a natural progression seems to be from gardening for birds to gardening for butterflies. Birds and butterflies share two very attractive things for a backyard enthusiast: they both fly and they both come in a dazzling array of different shapes, sizes, and colors. However, gardening for butterflies is a bit different from gardening for birds. Butterflies are creatures that are much more dependent on plants for their life cycle than are birds. When considering planting a butterfly garden, there are two types of plants that you need to consider. The first and perhaps most obvious are the nectar-bearing plants, which attract the adult butterflies and sometimes the hummingbirds in your area. These plants include, but are not limited to, Black-eyed Susan, Blazing Star, Butterfly Bush, Coreopsis, Joe-Pye Weed, Lantana, Mexican Sunflower, milkweed, pentas, Purple Coneflower, Salvia, and Zinnia. These plants provide nectar for butterflies and hummingbirds as well as seeds for the birds in the fall.

The native Joe-Pye Weed, *Eupatorium purpureum*

The other and most commonly overlooked plantings for butterflies are the host plants that provide food for the butterfly caterpillars, without which you can't get butterflies. Certain species of butterfly prefer specific host plants. The Monarch Butterfly caterpillars are most often found feeding on milkweed. Painted Ladies prefer to feed on thistle or hollyhock. The Mourning Cloak is most often found feeding on willows, elms, and birches. Black Swallowtails and Anise Swallowtails love Dill and Parsley. The Queen Butterfly's caterpillars, found in the southern United States, feed on milkweed; the Red Admiral's caterpillars feed on nettles.

Butterflies are an integral part of our environment, providing pollination for a great many plant species. They are also some of the most beautiful creatures that can visit your yard. Set aside an area for them in your garden. You will be pleased with the results.

The bright orange flowers of the milkweed known as Butterfly Weed draw more than their share of butterflies and also add an unusual color to the flower garden. Remember to plant flowers that bloom into the autumn, such as Cosmos, to help feed migrating butterflies.

The Birds

The following is a sampling of common birds that often find suitable habitat in backyard settings. Use this as a starting point for research into basic habitat requirements and behavioral observations; consult a field guide for more information on these and similar species of other regions. The diversity of birds is tremendous, with over 700 species found across North America. The birds shown here are fairly typical of backyard birds in the northeastern U. S. In the West, South, and Southwest you may find distinct species with similar requirements. Remember to familiarize yourself with the local birds before doing any habitat modification.

House Finch (*Carpodacus mexicanus*): If the term omnipresent could be applied to one bird, it would probably be the House Finch. Found regularly in cities, suburbs, farms, and just about anywhere else. It does, however, prefer the forest edge habitat and avoids denser woods.

American Goldfinch (*Carduelis tristis*): The American Goldfinch can be found in brushy patches of weeds along roadsides and the edges of woods. Often found eating the seeds of the heads of sunflowers, Globe Thistle, and Purple Coneflower.

Pine Siskin (*Carduelis pinus*): Prefers coniferous forests or mixed woodlands, especially those featuring alders. During winter months can be found with American Goldfinch, foraging for seed in dead weeds.

Common Redpoll (*Carduelis flammea*): Found in thickets and brushy areas in the northern part of North America. Especially fond of birches. During harsh northern winters can be found foraging with its close relatives—the House Finch, goldfinches, and Pine Siskin.

Purple Finch (*Carpodacus purpureus*): Often confused with its more cosmopolitan cousin the House Finch, the Purple Finch shares some of the habitat requirements of most finches. Prefers to live in mixed woods, especially those surrounding northern suburbs. Prefers building its nests in coniferous trees. In the western states, Purple Finch will breed in oaks and along streams.

Northern Cardinal (*Cardinalis cardinalis*): The bird that is all but synonymous with birdfeeding in the eastern two-thirds of the United States is a woodland edge-dweller. Can also be found in desert washes, especially those with Mesquite trees, where its range begins to spread into the Southwest. Prefers dense undergrowth for nesting.

Blue Jay (*Cyanocitta cristata*): This raucous member of the crow family can be found in oak and pine forest over better than two-thirds of the United States. Prefers mixed woods to breed in and is especially fond of stands of oak, due in large part to its love of acorns.

AMERICAN CROW (*CORVUS BRACHYRHYNCHOS*): An incredibly adaptable bird that can be found in many areas, including farms, fields, suburbs, and even cities. Prefers to breed in large trees, high off the ground. Their nests are often usurped by Great Horned Owls.

BLACK-CAPPED CHICKADEE (*POECILE ATRICAPILLUS*)
Prefers mixed woods; fond of willow thickets and shade trees, especially alders and birch trees. They will gladly move into your backyard, as long as proper nesting accommodations are made.
CAROLINA CHICKADEE (*POECILE CAROLINENSIS*)
The southern cousin of the Black-capped Chickadee shows a strong preference to streambank woodlands, especially those heavy in deciduous trees. Can be enticed into the suburbs by providing the proper trees and nesting sites.

CHESTNUT-BACKED CHICKADEE (*POECILE RUFESCENS*): This western chickadee prefers moist coniferous woodlands in the northern end of its range, while at the southern end they can be found in mixed woods, especially those with alders, willows, and oaks.

TUFTED TITMOUSE (*BAEOLOPHUS BICOLOR*)
A second cousin to the chickadees, the Tufted Titmouse has very similar habitat requirements. Prefers tall stands of deciduous trees. The Tufted Titmouse is a cavity- nester that will take advantage of a properly deployed nesting box.
OAK TITMOUSE (*BAEOLOPHUS INORNATUS*)
The Oak Titmouse lives up to its name, preferring to live in stands of oak trees, often along streambanks and forest edges. The Oak Titmouse is quite adaptable and thrives where yards provide essential habitat.

Downy Woodpecker (*Picoides nuttallii*): This is a common woodpecker that can find food from many sources, from dead weeds and seedpods of trees to suet feeders in backyards. Like all woodpeckers, dead and dying trees are crucial parts of its habitat.

Hairy Woodpecker (*Picoides villosus*): Similar to the Downy except for size and length of bill, both larger, the Hairy Woodpecker is adaptable to all types of habitat. Can be found in backyards with a surfeit of large trees.

Red-bellied Woodpecker (*Melanerpes carolinus*): Originally found in the Southeast, but has expanded its range in recent years. Prefers deciduous forest or mixed woodlands. The Red-bellied Woodpecker is especially fond of wet areas such as rivers and swamps; known to use large nesting boxes mounted high on trees.

Red-breasted Nuthatch (*Sitta canadensis*): Prefers to make its home in pine forests, but can also be found in deciduous trees as the weather cools. A cavity-nester that most often nests in spruce, fir, or hemlock trees.

White-breasted Nuthatch (*Sitta carolinensis*): Habitat preference is for a mature forest, primarily deciduous trees and sometimes in a mixed woodland. A woodland edge-dweller that can be coaxed into using nesting boxes.

Carolina Wren (*Thryothorus ludovicianus*): As with most of its relatives, prefers tangles and brush piles. A wren's habitat requirement should read the "messier the better."

House Wren (*Troglodytes aedon*): A very familiar backyard bird, with its loud, seemingly incessant call from low scrub and heavy underbrush. Those having a hard time attracting birds to nesting boxes should focus their efforts on these birds; they are more than happy to use most any dwelling provided.

The bright red foliage and clusters of fruits mark Smooth Sumac, a good but untidy bird planting.

Chapter Six

Working With Mother Nature

Lovingly neglecting your yard, or parts of it, is one of the easiest ways to enhance your bird habitat. Nature is funny that way. Leave it alone and it will do things that will amaze you. Berry-producing plants start popping up (seeds are "planted" by the birds that eat the berries). Brush piles and scrubby areas create themselves. Even sunflowers may start to grow.

In eliminating or reducing your weeding, pruning, and use of chemical controls, you must of course keep the concerns of your neighbors in mind. The back of your property along a fence or hidden corners of the yard are perhaps preferable to the front of your house—at least at first. If you are fortunate enough to live on such a large piece of land that neighbors are not an issue, let Mother Nature have a good portion of your backyard. Watch it slowly but surely return to a meadow over the years. Cut a path through it so you can enjoy it, and use the area to enhance other habitat elements such as feeders and water features.

Mother Nature's recuperative powers are awesome to behold, and within a couple years the bounty of your lack of labor will be yours for the enjoying. Give it a try and watch the results grow.

Snags and Dying Trees

Part of letting nature have its way is to let things die. Death is an integral part of nature, providing bounty for countless other living creatures, and it is the last curve in the great circle of life. Let plants that grow naturally in your yard go to seed. This will provide a supply of natural food for birds and other animals. Let trees die. As long as they pose no threat of falling on someone's home, let them die and decay naturally. There is more life going on in a dead tree than in a live one. Many birds and other creatures count on dead and dying trees for homes. One reason that humans have found a need for putting up nest boxes in our backyards is due primarily to the lack of dead and dying trees. Woodpeckers excavate their nest sites in dead trees. After they are done with them, these holes are used by secondary cavity-nesters, such as chickadees, titmice, nuthatches, Great Crested Flycatchers, and wrens. Dead trees also attract a great many insects that provide food for the wildlife in your backyard.

If you don't have any dead or dying trees in your backyard, "plant" one. Check with a local tree service or find a downed tree yourself. Find a good spot for it, dig a hole (at least one-third the length of the tree section itself) in the ground, stand it up, and then backfill the dirt. You can even drill some one-inch holes in the tree and fill them with suet to feed woodpeckers and other suet-loving birds. Who knows? Perhaps a woodpecker will excavate a nesting hole in it one spring.

It is worth mentioning that the absolutly worst time to start trimming, cutting, and removing vegetation from a yard is during the spring and early summer. At this time the odds of ruining a bird's nesting site increase a thousand fold. This is breeding season, a time of year of very high stress for birds. Each year stories are told of

GO WILD

One facet of habitat enhancement requires virtually no work on your part. Let part of your yard—a back corner or along a fence—go wild. Don't cut it, don't prune it, don't spray it, and don't plant anything, just let it go. Sit back and watch what happens over the next couple of years. Your native sparrow population will increase and you will be visited by some new and unfamiliar species. One of a bird's biggest predicaments is how to live in and survive on our overworked yards and gardens. We have a love affair with the sterile green patch called the lawn. In truth, this type of "monoculture" is unsuitable not only for birds but for many other forms of wildlife. It is also a very high maintenance undertaking, requiring exorbitant amounts of water and far too many chemical additives to maintain.

Snags and dying trees are important features of any bird-friendly habitat, and they have many uses for a variety of birds. The Acorn Woodpecker, for instance, places acorns into a pattern of drilled holes in the trunks and branches of trees, assuring a food supply for the winter. As old trees disappear, birds often disappear with them.

homeowners cutting down trees or limbs only to find cavity-nesting birds in the removed segment. The only hope for these homeless birds is to take them to the nearest federally licensed rehabilitation center.

Brush Piles

Another valuable addition to your backyard sanctuary is a simple pile of brush—an accumulation of downed limbs and branches, several years' worth of Christmas trees, and any other piece of woodland debris you can come up with. This is by far one of the easiest and most effective ways of creating cover for your backyard birds. When predators or other threats enter your yard, watch how the birds will make a hasty rush for your brush pile. Not only birds appreciate brush piles; so do chipmunks, squirrels, field mice, and many other animals.

Dust baths

Certain species of birds, such as pheasants, quails, wild turkey, thrashers, wrens, sparrows, and even the occasional bird of prey, have been known to wallow around in the dust. The dust gets in between their feathers, increasing their loft and thereby their ability to insulate. It also can drastically cut down on the number of

A neat brush pile provides cover for birds all year and does not have to be an eye-sore.

CHRISTMAS IN JULY

If you are someone who gets a fresh cut tree every Christmas, don't drag it out to the curb once you are finished with it this year. Position it somewhere near your feeders and watch the birds use it as a staging area before landing on your feeders. They'll seek shelter from foul weather within its boughs, even after the last of the needles have fallen off and the batteries have died in the last of the new toys.

parasites living on them. Birds prefer very fine dirt for their bathing, sometimes even sand. If you care to provide such a "bath" for your birds, dig a hole deep enough to accommodate approximately 6 inches of "dust." You can create your own dust mix by combining one-third sand, one-third ash, and one-third loam. Surround the area with some natural rocks or logs to keep your dust bath intact.

Nesting Materials

You can supply birds with nesting materials by recycling a variety of household items. Hair from your hairbrush or from your dogs or cats can be put out, as can lint from the clothes dryer. However, if you are going to provide this lint, be certain that you do not use fabric softener sheets in the dryer; these are full of chemicals that may be hazardous to birds and their nestlings. Odd pieces of string and yarn, cotton from medicine bottles, and many other things can be used as nesting material. In fact, the House Sparrow, not necessarily a bird you wish to encourage to nest in your yard, has been known to use almost anything in its nest—cigarette filters, cellophane wrappers, even yards of cassette tape.

Keep in mind that anything you put out should be free of chemicals. When in doubt of the safety of something, always err on the side of the birds.

You will not draw woodpeckers to your backyard during the summer if you do not have suitable nesting trees nearby. Here a Hairy Woodpecker looks out from its nesthole.

Go Natural

Although it has been mentioned earlier, it is so important that it bears mentioning again. When tending to your enhanced habitat, please avoid the use of pesticides and other unnatural products. Many nurseries and garden centers feature products that are completely safe for birds and other wildlife. Talk to your

A backyard that is suitable for birds also is suitable for a variety of other animals, some enjoyable, some pesty. Prepare yourself to live with groundhogs (woodchucks), squirrels, chipmunks, and even the occasional deer and raccoon. All are deserving of your attention.

nursery expert about how to have an attractive and safe backyard for yourself and your visitors.

Extending the Invitation

As you create your bird-friendly environment, please keep in mind that by sustaining a healthy bird population in your yard you will be inviting other guests as well. Squirrels, deer, opossums, raccoons, groundhogs, chipmunks, mice, and other creatures may find your yard an oasis in a concrete desert. It is important to remember that these too are wild creatures running out of places to live. Welcome these creatures to your yard. Accept them as a sign that you have created a truly fine habitat in your little corner of the world and appreciate them all.

Enjoy!

One of the nicest things about birdfeeding, birdwatching, and the other activities that go with them is that they can be done to suit your own level of comfort. If you want to re-landscape ten acres into your own little recreation of a great eastern forest, go for it. It may take a generation or two to come around, but why not? Then again, if you are more comfortable planting one new flower for butterflies or hummingbirds each spring, that's great too. Every little bit helps, and every little bit can attract more birds into your backyard. Enjoy!

RESOURCES

Cornell Lab of Ornithology

MEMBERSHIP DEPARTMENT

P.O. Box 11
Ithaca, NY 14851
www.ornith.cornell.edu
A membership institute whose mission is to interpret and conserve the earth's biodiversity through research, education, and citizen science based on birds.

National Audubon Society

700 Broadway
New York, NY 10003
www.audubon.org
The mission of the National Audubon Society is to conserve and restore natural ecosystems, focusing on birds and other wildlife for the benefit of humanity and the earth's biological diversity.

National Wildlife Federation

BACKYARD WILDLIFE HABITAT™

8925 Leesburg Pike
Vienna, VA 22184
www.nwf.org/habitat
NWF's backyard habitat program aids and encourages landscaping with the needs of wildlife and the health of the environment in mind.

The Natural Lands Trust

HILDACY FARM

1031 Palmers Mill Road
Media, PA 19063
www.natlands.org
A nonprofit regional land trust working to protect natural areas in Pennsylvania.

The Xerces Society

10 Southwest Ash Street
Portland, OR 97204
www.xerces.org
An international nonprofit organization focused on public education about invertebrates and conservation projects that demonstrate their critical role in endangered ecosystems.

Magazines and Periodicals

BIRDER'S WORLD

P.O. Box 1612
Waukesha, WI 53187-1612
1-800-446-5489

BIRD WATCHER'S DIGEST

P.O. Box 110
Marietta, OH 45750
1-800-879-2473

WILDBIRD

Subscription Department
P.O. Box 52898
Boulder, CO 80323-2898

Feeder Manufacturers & Retailers

DROLL YANKEES

Foster, RI

ARUNDALE PRODUCTS

Mandarin Feeders

BACKYARD NATURE PRODUCTS/ BIRD STUFF/WOOD COUNTRY

Chilton, WI

C&S PRODUCTS

HEATH FEEDERS AND FEED

WILD BIRD CENTERS OF AMERICA

Glen Echo, MD

Optics for Birding

LEICA CAMERA: 1-800-222-0118

NIKON: 1-800-NIKON-US

SWAROVSKI OPTIK

SWIFT INSTRUMENTS: 1-800-446-1116

Organizations

NEW JERSEY AUDUBON SOCIETY

9 Hardscrabble Rd.
Bernardsville, NJ 07924
1-908-766-5787

AMERICAN BIRDING ASSOCIATION

P.O. Box 6599
Colorado Springs, CO 80934
1-719-578-1614
www.americanbirding.org

INDEX

Page numbers in **bold** indicate photos